FIELD TRIPS

The Farm

Stuart A. Kallen
ABDO & Daughters

Published by Abdo & Daughters, 4940 Viking Drive, Suite 622, Edina, Minnesota 55435.

Printed in the United States.

Cover and Interior Photo credits: Peter Arnold, Inc.
Archive Photos
Wide World Photos

Illustration: Ben Dann Lander
Edited by Julie Berg

Library of Congress Cataloging-in-Publication Data

Kallen, Stuart A., 1955-
The farm / Stuart A. Kallen.
p. cm. — (Field trips)
Includes index.
Summary: Describes the crops, animals, equipment, and routine life on a family farm.
ISBN 1-56239-713-3
1. Agriculture—Juvenile literature. 2. Farms—Juvenile literature. 3. Farm life—Juvenile literature. [1. Agriculture. 2. Farms. 3. Farm life.] I. Title. II. Series.
S519.K35 1997
630—dc20 96-9191
CIP
AC

Contents

Where Food Comes From

Grocery stores are full of food. There's meat, fruit, vegetables, and bread. Bottles, cans, and packages hold every food you can think of. There's cereal, steak, and spaghetti. But where does all this food come from?

Farms, of course. You'll see where all that delicious food comes from when you take a field trip to a farm.

Let's look at what makes up a pizza. It contains many farm products. The crust is made from wheat grown in a farm field. The tomato sauce, peppers, and onions are vegetables grown on a farm. The sausage is made from pigs raised on a farm.

We wouldn't have any food to eat without farms and farmers.

Opposite page: Grocery stores are full of food grown on farms.

59 Ea.
Harvest Fresh

Planting the Crops

Food comes from plants called **crops**. When you go to a farm, you'll see where the farmers have plowed up the **soil**, planted seeds, and **harvested** the crop after it has grown.

While the crops are growing, the farmer must kill weeds and **fertilize** the plants. Giant machines help the farmer with this work.

Farmers grow wheat, barley, soy beans, corn, and vegetables. They grow hay for cows, sheep, and horses. Farmers also grow strawberries, broccoli, onions, beans, and other fruits or vegetables.

The type of food farmers grow depends on where they live. In warm places, farmers may grow fruit and vegetables. In cold places, farmers may grow grain, barley, and soy beans. Farms that do not use **chemicals** to grow their plants are called **organic farms**.

Farmers plow the field before they plant.

Milking the Cows

Along with growing **crops** some farmers raise **dairy** cows. Cows give us milk. Milk can be made into cheese, cottage cheese, yogurt, cream cheese, and other products. Milking cows is hard work and farmers must do it two times every day. They can't even take a day off for Christmas!

Cows are milked with special equipment. First they are guided into special barn stalls. They are given food in long **troughs** during milking so they stay calm. While the cows are eating grain, farmers wash the **udders** with special soap. Then, automatic milking machines are put on the udders.

Rich, creamy milk is drawn through plastic tubes into large bottles. Then the milk flows into a **refrigerated** tank.

Two people can milk 55 cows using milking equipment. Every other day, a large tanker truck pulls into the farm

and takes the milk away to one day be bottled and sold to stores.

Maybe you'll get to help the farmer milk his cows. Don't be afraid. Cows are used to people working with them.

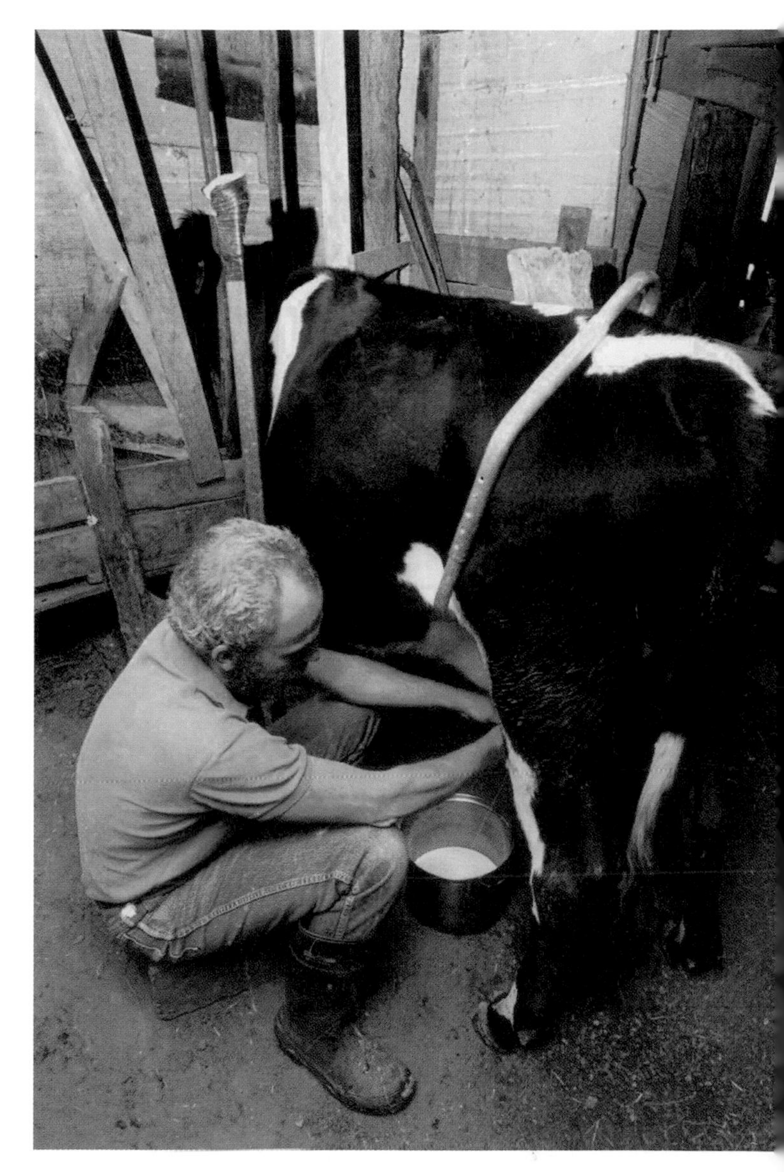

This dairy farmer must milk his cows two times every day.

Farm Animals

Farmers raise many kinds of animals. Chickens are raised for meat and eggs. Pigs are raised for ham, pork chops and other meats. Sheep are raised for wool. Sometimes a farmer has goats for milk. Turkeys are raised for Thanksgiving dinner!

You will see many baby animals on a farm. Baby cows are called calves. They need to be fed, cleaned, and cared for. They love to have their noses rubbed.

Baby sheep are called lambs. They're so soft. Baby pigs are called piglets. If you pick one up, they'll squeak and squeal. Baby chickens are called chicks. All are cute and cuddly. But soon they will grow up to be adult farm animals.

Other farmers have horses, ponies, and donkeys. In the old days, these animals pulled plows. Today, farmers use tractors instead of horses. But you can feed carrots to the horses. You might even get to ride them.

This farmer raises pigs to be sold as ham in stores.

Farm Machines

Giant farm machines are big, loud, and sometimes dangerous. But without machines, farmers could not grow enough food to feed everybody.

Tractors pull plows and wagons, and spread **fertilizer**. Giant **combines harvest** the **crops**. **Front-end loaders** shovel grain and pick up huge **bales** of hay. **Balers** pick up cut hay in the field and make bales. Pickup trucks haul smaller things. Large trucks haul hay and animals.

When it doesn't rain enough for the crops to grow, some farmers use giant watering pipes to **irrigate** their fields. These machines move through the fields and spray water on crops. Sometimes farmers use water from streams and rivers to fill irrigation ditches between rows of crops.

Farm machines are very expensive. A combine may cost as much as a house!

Farmers must fix machinery that breaks. A **crop** may be lost if machinery breaks down during a **harvest**.

Big machines help farmers do hard work faster.

THE FARM
crops
W
N
S
E

silo
barn

Life on the Farm

Farming is hard work. Many farmers work from five o'clock in the morning until nine o'clock at night.

Everybody works on a farm. Moms and dads drive tractors, fix machines, and cook meals. Kids do chores like picking weeds and feeding animals. Even the pets help out. Dogs **herd** sheep and cows into the barn. Cats catch mice that get into the **silos**.

Many farmers have a vegetable garden where they grow food for their own use. If you visit a vegetable garden you might see peas, broccoli, tomatoes, and peppers.

Opposite page: Some farmers handpick their crops.

Farm Kids

Maybe you'll meet kids like you who live on the farm. But life is different for farm kids. They must get up in the morning and milk the cows. Then they do chores and eat breakfast. After that they must go to school all day! After school, kids have to milk the cows again.

In the summer, kids walk through fields picking large weeds. This is called "walking the beans." The weeds will jam the **combine** if they aren't pulled.

Some farm kids are in the 4-H Club. Kids raise special animals for 4-H contests. Prizes are given for the best pig, horse, chicken, sheep, and other animals.

Farming isn't all work for kids. Sometimes they get to swim, ride horses, run through the woods, and play.

Opposite page: These farm kids are gathering eggs.

Living By Nature

Farmers depend on nature to survive. Regular rain is needed to water the **crops**. But it must be dry in early spring so the farmer can drive large machines in the fields to plant. Cold weather can kill growing crops. Hail can turn a healthy cornfield into a total loss. Many times the weather is not right for growing.

Farmers live by the seasons. The fields lay under a blanket of snow in winter. In spring they are raked smooth, plowed, and planted. In the summer rows of corn are weeded. During the fall, crops are **harvested**.

When the sun goes down the farm gets quiet. Everybody is tired from working hard. The kids are in bed and the crickets chirp in the fields. When the sun comes up tomorrow, it all starts again.

Visit a farm. You'll get to see what life is like for people who put food on your table.

Opposite page:
Winter on the farm.

Glossary

bales (BAY-ulz) - large bundles of straw wrapped for storage.

baler (BAY-ler) - a machine that bales hay.

chemical (KEM-ih-kull) - acids, bases, and gases such as oxygen and hydrogen.

combine - a machine used for cutting grain.

crops - plants grown for feeding people and animals.

dairy - having to do with milk and products made from milk.

fertilizer (FUR-tuh-lie-zer) - material used to make plants grow better.

front-end loader - a machine with a shovel on the front.

harvest - to pick crops after they are done growing.

herd - to tend or take care of cattle or sheep.

irrigation (ear-uh-GAY-shun) - to supply land with water using streams or machinery.

organic farm - farms where crops and animals are raised without the use of chemicals like weed and insect killers.

refrigerated (ree-FRIJ-er-ray-ted) - kept cold like a refrigerator.

silo - a tall, round building in which green food for farm animals can be stored without spoiling.

soil - dirt.

troughs (TRAWFS) - long, narrow containers for holding food or water.

udder - the gland on a cow that makes milk.

Index